DISPATCHES FROM THE MEMORY CARE MUSEUM

DISPATCHES FROM THE MEMORY CARE MUSEUM

Poetry by

Mary K O'Melveny

Kelsay Books

Cover photograph: Mary K O'Melveny
Cover concepts: Elizabeth Anastasia O'Melveny

ISBN: 978-1-954353-82-4

Kelsay Books
502 South 1040 East, A-119
American Fork, Utah, 84003

DISPATCHES FROM THE MEMORY CARE MUSEUM

TABLE OF CONTENTS

PART I:

DISPATCHES FROM
THE MEMORY CARE MUSEUM

PART II: GOINGS AND COMINGS

PART III:

THROUGH THE LOOKING GLASS

PART IV:

WHO WILL BEAR THE WEIGHT OF WHAT WE HAVE KNOWN?

For Frances, Randy and all those whose memories shape-shifted but never left us in doubt about how they touched our lives.

The light of memory, or rather the light that memory lends to things, is the palest light of all. I am not quite sure whether I am dreaming or remembering, whether I have lived my life or dreamed it.

— Eugene Ionesco

PART I:

DISPATCHES FROM
THE MEMORY CARE MUSUEM

In time of crisis, we summon up our strength. Then, if we are lucky, we are able to call every resource, every forgotten image that can leap to our quickening, every memory that can make us know our power.

— **Muriel Rukeyser**

DISPATCHES FROM
THE MEMORY CARE MUSEUM

What did we know
and when did we know it?

Imagine all the metal
cabinets of a mind
filled with fragments
of missing hours and days.
Each locked away from visitors –
a dull gemstone that might
still glow in certain light,
a furred paw, some browned
teeth, a catfish carcass,
trading beads that sealed
some ancient land deal,
baskets of braided
sweetgrass, an ink drawing
of a long extinct bird,
soft rustle of feathers
almost audible, a map
of ancient alleyways,
an abacus, a rusted hourglass.

Someone misplaced the keys.
We open a new drawer.

1

THOUGHTS ON MEMORY'S VISCOSITY

*A viscous fluid flows very slowly. Viscosity results from a fluid's internal friction caused when molecules are moved against each other. Applied force reduces the tendency to flow freely and disperse quickly. In glassblowing, a gaffer is the person who uses a blowpipe to inflate molten glass into a bubble. A punty is the metal rod used at the end of the blowing process. The gather is the portion of glass that has spooled at one end of the blowpipe after short puffs of air have been blown into it. Once the glass has been blown to near its intended size, the rod, tipped with a wad of hot glass, is attached to the bottom of the vessel to hold it in place while the top portion is completed.

We mourn each loss. Want time solid
like a glass beaker. We want to be
gaffers, to inflate each bubble
with air, turn our blowpipe toward fire.
As our gather fills, it spools thick
ribbons encircling a molten cloud.
Each new layer expands memory
until interior matches exterior.
We press our punty toward furnace,
flame. Each moment salvaged, then sealed.
Soon, nothing will slip past us.
Burdens we did not want will melt
away. Our vessel translucent.
As it hardens, we remember
what pleased us. What took our breath away.

WHAT IF EACH FALLING LEAF WAS
SOMETHING WE WANTED TO REMEMBER?

The lawn burns with hues of red, gold,
russet, green. Each leaf unique,
as if emigrés with checkered pasts
had wandered into my yard.
With each step, an acorn mast
creates risk of a turned ankle, yet I
march forward, look past the downpour
into slanted light of the far woods.
There, oak, hickory and black maple
shed their thoughts as I watch. If
each falling fragment had been spun
from the forest of my mind, what
would I find? A hint of white heat here,
some sugar-tinged moment there. A flash
of crimson heartache. A dark stain of regret.
A time when my world was cleansed
by diffused light. A time when water
spilled, when optimism shriveled
like droppings from elms. Another
when spare branches were all I could see.

IN THE END, WHAT DO WE WANT TO KNOW?

My mother never forgot our names.
What she often forgot was that we
were once loveable. That we loved her.

As memory melts away, I have marveled at
what elects to bubble up against odds
of wish or will, lacking prediction or point

of view. Each day, we never knew which
grains would cling to her cerebral
colander or wash away, perhaps

forever, perhaps until tomorrow's
new light slanted toward them once more,
as her thoughts rose like newly kneaded dough.

As we searched for order or, failing that,
predictability of loss, it was often her anger
that remained constant. Sometimes her fury

at time's passage was so pure it resembled
monastic prayer. *How did this happen?*
Why is it over before I could make sense

of anything? And then, just as suddenly,
she would smile, metallic taste of outrage
replaced by something new, nearly sweet.

the source of every argument

is the memory of
the last one
that scorched us
as if we had
stuck our hands
into the fire
forgetting the
sear of burned flesh
watching it burn
turn to cinders

a child
unconceived
or abandoned
a debt unpaid
faith discarded
for false gods
or fool's errands
failure to believe
letters unread
or steamed open

eventually
someone douses
water on flames
we stumble back
to civil discourse
snuff out our
unresolved complaints
stuff them back
to some brain recess
until ashes ignite anew

this is why wars never end
how reparations are never paid
we cannot forget
or forgive or move on

try to find higher ground
a brief caress soothes
until we brush it off
in favor of furies so pure
we always return
to worship at their altar

DIAGNOSIS

I
Amyloid betas
and beta amyloids,
taus and prions,
neurofibrillary tangles.
Rogue proteins all,
they swim, float upward, dance
like a disordered nebula,
a spiral galaxy.
As if Joan Miró
or Paul Klee
had been painting
on her brain.

Here is when we want
Rembrandts, Courbets,
Vermeers, Tintorellos.
Solid, lush and finely wrought,
thick with meaning,
nothing lost. Morning light
bends in from a window,
pearl earrings glow,
an apple shines against
a velvet cloth, layers of
paint glow with depth,
details intact.

II
She began her search
for lost words carefully,
as if cultivating
some rare plant
in her greenhouse.
At first, it was like
a botany project—
roots and seeds all there,
she just needed time

to divide, fertilize,
reassemble. Eventually
the thought blossomed up.
Later on, she learned
to leave them fallow,

live without. New words
germinated instead,
close in sound, size,
round and vibrant.
Some were overripe.
Others sprouted quickly,
turned bright in sunshine.
They filled the void.
She let others guess at meanings,
like a parlor game.

III

She stands in silence
by the kitchen doorway.
Her apple trees are lush with fruit.
The pond gleams in the day's late light.
Her vegetable beds have thinned down.
She can still isolate weeds, pull them.
Some tasks so ingrained, after all,
they are like circulating blood.
She knows what grew there.
As a chill rises, she walks away,
satisfied with her simple work,
walks to her son's memory garden.

It has shifted now to palest shades,
a resting place for falling leaves.
A weathered wind chime still hangs there,
its sound lingers, soft and clean.
She no longer recalls his death.
It is more an ache. Stark shouting
edges of her great grief are muffled,
as if she has cushioned a broken arm

8

in a warm fleece blanket. She knows
that he is gone but what she recalls is
a sweet boy she once knew who raced
horses with her along a summer meadow.

IV
Eventually, days lose margins.
People disappear Giacometti-like,
even in daylight. Dali predominates.
Twombly scribbles across a faded canvas.
Lush impressionistic images
give way to Pollack,
Rothko, Serra, Still.
A nimbus of loss remains.
As color cools,
she is diaphanous.

TRAVELS TO THE VALLEY OF LOST THINGS

*Orlando Furioso was the titled hero of a romantic epic poem by
Ludovio Ariosto, first published in 1516 and written in a rhyming
stanza format known as *ottava rima*. Orlando, one of Charlemagne's
knights, goes mad when the woman he loves betrays him. His friend
Astolpho, another knight, flies to the moon – where it is said all
missing things can be found – in search of Orlando's wits. In the
original poem, Orlando's wits are recovered. Five hundred years later,
no cure has been found for dementia.

It is said all missing things
might end up on the moon –
the royal battle gear of kings,
lesser leavings too – cups and spoons,
missing teeth or spectacles, slings
and arrows of heartbreak strewn
about like poetry fragments, ill-fated
once they left a lover unpersuaded.

My best friend's mind flew to pieces
like Orlando Furioso's. Flying
in a fiery chariot to that orbed precipice,
I became Astolfo. I sought clarifying
memories I hoped might well free us
both if we retrieved their edifying
truths. I feared they would be hidden
on the moon's dark side – forbidden

fruit for searchers who would rather
snatch up bits of sound, pretend they mean
something more than random blather.
If thoughts were stones, it seems
heft alone might assist a gatherer
bent on carrying home some gleam
of truth. Like a necklace breaking,
her cognition scattered to ground. Raking

thoughts back up like so many grains
of sand proved too difficult, despite

my zeal. It seems what is lost remains
so. Even my struggles with hindsight,
scattered throughout these lunar domains,
yielded little. I wanted to ignite
those flames of recollection needed
to return to lucid orbits that preceded

her collapsing persona. My intended
quest is doomed even on this landscape
rich with absent details. Nothing my friend did
or said can be unearthed in any shape
or form here. At last, I apprehended
how hope fades. While I groped and gaped
at cerebral debris, even moonlight
had disappeared from her line of sight.

WORD SEARCH

no one could quite recall
when it first began
like a faucet drip
so small a drop
no one pays attention
so soft   so thin
like ribbons of daylight
before dawn spools outward
or winter storms that begin
with just a few flakes
drifting onto grass
silent as barefoot thieves

a word wanders away
hides inside other sounds
it teases her   flirts
she hopes it will
hop back into her lap
any moment now
bask in her happiness
at how she avoided
the rigors of confession
the dirty business of
offering apologies
for losing her trail
of thoughts   when tracking
them down feels so hard

soon enough she grows tired
of searching   learns to build
a brand new language
from tattered bits and hints
a foal of bapples a scarry shy
when a missing meaning
turns up unannounced
she welcomes it home
like an old friend

words to a childhood hymn
arrive unbidden
she doesn't mind surprises
she is thrilled to sing along
we join her when we can

DO EMPTY SPACES MAKE THE STORY?

*In 2014, the American Psychological Association released a study, *The Benefits of Forgetting*. Researchers concluded that forgetting certain things could be advantageous (even though "the benefits of excellent memory are obvious") because we rely on memory for such things as "remembering the grocery list, a colleague's name or the location of the car keys." However, "forgetting can be beneficial for real-world associative learning. Multiple cues may be present in the environment at any given time, even if they do not have a meaningful relationship. Thus, successful learning involves both learning true relationships and forgetting random relationships that do not have predictive value." Forgetting is beneficial for creative thinking, they concluded, because it can make "information that is no longer useful less accessible, so it does not interfere with access to new information or clues."

We let go of things
we no longer need to know
to make bigger, better decisions.
So say scientists who study
human brains. Our cerebral
red editorial pen cancels
out thoughts we once held,
propels us toward shrewdness.

Good memories do not need
the clutter of details: where we left
our keys or names of former
colleagues. Our brains might burst
if overfilled with every email,
random route or telephone number.
Prize-winning novels or sonatas
for strings and piano need space

to emerge to light. A Hippocampus
filled with minor verse harbors
no room for epic poems. Each slight
recalled, each still focused sight,
shrouds unspoken visions. Yet,
we find it hard to shed the weight

of words, nuzzle into each phrase
of quarrels like the fur of a family pet.

We stroke each meaning, store
notes and nuance deep in cerebrum
cortex. They doze there waiting,
dreaming of chase. When the next
argument blows in like a tropical
storm ready to be named, they emerge,
fine-tuned, easy to deploy.

Not everyone is good at Cerebellum
gardening. Some hope rhizomes will
sprout in each new sentence. But
others see that what goes missing
is not always worth keeping. Erasures
need not undo us. There can be solace
in silences. Sometimes, we misplace car keys
because we do not want to go home.

THE FIFTH DIMENSION

There is a crack in everything.
That's how the light gets in.

——Leonard Cohen

As I was talking to my friend, he broke
down in tears, recalling anew, that his
wife had recently died. Is gone. Today,
some telemarketer asked to speak to
my long dead mother. For one tiny tick
of a clock, I almost handed her the phone.

How do we navigate shape-shifting grief
and still make coffee in the morning,
exchange words with neighbors about the
sorry state of our televised world or look out
our windows to gauge if promised rain
might fade to something akin to mist?

Surely, it is in those split seconds when
memory's failure blots out bereavement,
when we step forward into some state of
transcendental mercy when yesterday
is restored. A slant of sunlight on snow.
Before the unthinkable had time

to be thought. Before we had to
don mourning garments or speak in past
tenses. Our ground solidifies.
A conversation continues. A smile
returns. We want to stay there,
liberated from known dimensions.

CONCENTRICITY

*Concentric circles are circles with a common center. In geometry, two or more objects are said to be concentric, coaxal, or coaxial when they share the same center or axis.

Grief is the inversion center.
All else is periphery.
Our loved ones die before we are
ready to lose them, leaving us
reaching for elusive ripples
of memory. We try to patch
together some montage that will
save us from despair's constancy.
Some central axis that can hold
against sorrow's tidal waves.
Rings of remorse fan out in all
directions even as we look
backwards in search of solace,
even as we try to measure
moments no longer tangible.
Now we have entered a stranger's
life. Different, yet parallel.
Survival just beyond our grasp.
As near and as far as starlight.
As wide and as deep as floodwaters.

THREE PM NEW YEAR'S EVE AT SUNSHINE VILLAGE

The guests are wearing paper hats
laced with rainbow streamers.
A sparkled ball clings to the ceiling.
Even those who thought themselves
long past it, cannot quite suppress a
smile as they grab fistfuls of noisemakers.

Those who can hurry toward plastic
chairs. Others, aided by wheels and
metal architecture, maneuver like
soldiers heading toward bivouac,
scout for ends of rows in case
early exit is required. A jazz trio

is setting up to play at the
front of the community room.
The piano player fingers the keys,
the bassist works his way down from
the neck, stretches his hands over
widening frets. The sax player
moistens his reeds, checks his music.

As the room fills, a long table is centered
by a punch bowl and paper cups. Ice dots
a salmon colored liquid like skiffs
on a lake turned sunset pink. At each end,
sheet cakes announce a dawning year in
Palmer scripted baby blue with sprinkles.

This is where unceremonious dreams
may end. Or begin anew. *Fly me
to the moon* croons the trio's leader
as everyone settles in for the ride.
*Satin doll. I can't give you anything
but love.* Everyone recalls the words.

A fine romance. The way you look tonight.
Memory is funny like that.
A light snaps on, focus shifts back
to love's first glow. Or heartbreak's slap.
Startled by the warmth of a June night
or the crack of ice in a whiskey glass.

PLAYING CARDS WITH MIRABELLE

Playing cards with Mirabelle,
my grandniece, the thrill of
young, lithe memory shines
against afternoon sunlight.
Agile. Innocent. Precise.
She takes only one glance
at neat rows of plastic
cards laid out before us
on the maple dining table
and she knows how her next
next round's picks will go.
Victory is assured, game after game.

She can spot each pair of snakes,
snow leopards, hippos, monkeys
like a seasoned zookeeper. I am
no match for her camera eye.
Soon we switch to a game
I did not know was still
played. *No one wants to be
the Old Maid,* she whispers.
She is barely six years old.
She cannot tell me why
an *Old Maid* is scary,
does not know what it means

to become one. Her parents
are divorcing. She is
just learning about a world
of two houses, changing
schedules, packed suitcases.
Her tidy memories
are still fresh, achingly pure.
She has much time to learn
there can be joy in being alone.

UNSUBSCRIBE

I spent time today
pushing and clicking
buttons and links.
All designed to
remove me
from commerce,
from conversations,
from cooking insights
and calico curtains.
From onslaughts,
opportunities
and outrages,
sordid tales
of dreams gone dim.

No one really
wanted me to leave.
Some begged me
to stick around.
Offered options.
Sought my opinion.
Were sorry to offend.
Wasn't it a simple
misunderstanding?
Wouldn't I consider
a brief reprieve?
There were causes
in need of rescue.
Consciences to be salved.

Suppose memory
worked this way.
We controlled what stayed
and what strayed away
from our grasp like unruly
children on a playground.

We were in charge of synapse,
neurotransmitters bent
to our will, molecules
waiting to bond with our
best moments, swim away
from mistakes and regrets.
We want veto power.
A second chance to get it right.

THINKING ABOT YOU

I asked "Alexa" how she was feeling.
She said *You know how you feel when
you write a poem and you think it's no good
and then you decide later that it's not too bad?*

I asked her again and she said
I'm not so sure. Maybe she meant she'd
changed her mind about the poem again.
I've felt that way sometimes.

Or maybe she was testing me. I'm quite
new to AI. "Siri" once chimed in during
a meeting of my writing group to say
I did not understand that. We laughed nervously.

Now I see that robots can care for
old folks. French elders have just met "Zora."
S/he/they/x is gender fluid. Apparently
ambiguity calms everyone down.

There are even puppy bots. You can
walk them outside with no need to clean
up afterwards. They bark, growl and sit.
They do not bite, smell or have fleas.

Maybe there is something to be said
for artificial friends. You can ask them
anything at all. No offense meant.
None taken. No harbored grievances

curled up in fetal positions
waiting to burst forth into your
quiet bedroom. Even the purity
of a *Good night* hangs briefly in

the air free of judgments
or missed opportunities.
Then the answer—clean, crisp, sure—
Good night. Sleep tight. As if your mother

had returned to tuck you in, peaceful
slumber soon to follow. Perhaps this is
meant to be. Algorithms instead of angst.
Sensory predictors instead of sentiment.

Simulated references. Virtual reality
free of messy memoired history.
Function is structure. Elon Musk trains
robots in imitation learning.

A one-stop system. Maybe neural
networks can be programmed
to light up whenever *kindness* occurs.
When memory has a chance to save us.

EARLY MARCH MORNING

As I stare out our window,
morning light lands, polished
as a museum jewel case.
Spare tree limbs hold a surprise.
Their pubescent buds, shaded
in pink, mauve, palest peach,
cling like baby tears
to each wakening branch.

A fringe of primal green
has settled around each
trunk like an intake of
breath before a song.
A chilled edge flirts with
warming air, yet it stays
lush, loamy, yielding
space for robin chorales.

Down at street level, a
woman pushes her cart
filled with bags of varied
forms and shapes. Her once-loved
treasures refuse to all
eyes but hers, where power
of memory irradiates
a broken china cat,
a scratched Duke Ellington
record. A tattered book
of sonnets raucous with
colors of expectation.

FAREWELLS

—For my friend Steve Moldof

It has been said that no grief goes
unrelieved. This worthy thought feels
true, even now in the thick of it.

Saying goodbye never comes easy.
Keening sounds reverberate in
the echo chambers of our distress.

Sadness can hover over us like
a murmuration of starlings while
we search for laughter like bird-watchers.

Each time we stare at a paper-strewn
desk or enter an emptied room,
we are startled anew by absence.

To help us navigate what remains,
we bulk up on memories like
veteran long distance runners.

Eventually, hearts will heal.
Instead of anguish over what we have lost,
we will be awed by what we were given.

PART II:

GOINGS AND COMINGS

A shadow is never created in darkness. It is born of light. We can be blind to it and blinded by it. Our shadow asks us to look at what we don't want to see.

——Terry Tempest Williams,
When Women Were Birds

MACULAR DEGENERATION

"What three things can never be done?
Forget. Keep silent. Stand alone.
The hill of glass, the fatal brilliant plain."

— **Muriel Rukeyser, The Book of the Dead**

I.
At first, fire flashes appeared
at a corner of sight, the way
a flame first catches paper's
edge, a soft curl of tan on white.

Later, the center shifted off like
a lazy cloud as sun sets, light
filtered past, settled elsewhere,
a blossoming sky still sweet enough.

Eventually, a kind of greyness
invaded faces we once knew well.
It interrupted our concentrations.
We squinted into the distance,

questioned yesterday's memories
as if we had never walked such paths
or sensed their dangers. We waited for
clarity to grace us once more.

II.
Perhaps we meant to speak up
when what we had always known
began to fade but imagined no one
else would recognize our losses.

Then, fearing missteps, we withdrew.
We blinked, pressed our rage back to
cortex corners, rolled out memories
from hippocampus hiding spots.

As we tried to focus on the
ways that vision can deceive us,
rafts overturned, gates clanged shut,
babies wept in box store cages,

others drowned in surging rivers,
waterways filled with poisons,
endangered species vanished.
Each time we looked, less remained.

BURIAL GROUNDS

*On the eve of the American Revolution, New York City had the
largest number of Africans of any English colonial settlement except
Charleston, South Carolina, and the highest proportion of slaves to
Europeans of any northern settlement. Africans and African Americans
were essential to New York's development. In 2007, the African Burial
Ground National Monument, at Duane and Elk Streets in Lower
Manhattan, commemorated their role in colonial and federal New York
City, and in United States history. It is thought that more than 15,000
people, both freed and enslaved, were buried at this site.

The dead lie beneath our feet.
Woods, grassy knolls, rolling hills,
a random yard. Sale of humans took place
on corners, county squares, dockyards,
even cathedral grounds – where prayers
rose from worshippers huddled
on oak benches in search of their
salvations. They whisper as we sleep,
graves marked by painted rocks, twigs,
granite stones. Crime victims all.

As we search like forensic experts,
we visit somber spaces where souls
stay shrouded even when we know
their names. In Poland, we tried to find
a vanished Jewish graveyard while a
scowling farmer pretended innocence,
ignorance. On Duane Street, fifteen
thousand Africans vanished into
service, sweat, soil. Each footfall
could dislodge athenaeums.

If we laid down on this ground,
what could we remember that would
rival the biographies resting here?
Like insomniacs in search of sleep,
we try to chronicle misfortunes
so grave that our own lives
will seem perfect. Or perhaps we

simply prefer the sheen of an
emerald lawn, a golden meadow,
a field of daisies white as cotton.

IN MEMORIAM FOR MEMORIALS

Once-jaunty ribbons mix
with plastic flowers and
long-dead petals, old gold
Mardi Gras bead strings, a
stuffed animal or two,
a few small coins, pennies
mostly, some heartfelt notes
and faded framed pictures.

The detritus of grief.
It is usually the photos
of dead children that get me.
Graduation caps and gowns,
white lace wedding dresses.
Sometimes a baptismal frock
or first communion suit,
hair slicked back, eyes bright.

Pop-up shrines swell. Their
faint sheen pulsates against
the gloom of crushing loss.
Doleful dolmens standing
in for the bereaved who
must attend to details
of death even though they would
prefer to lie weeping here.

It won't be long, one thinks,
before thoroughfares will
jam up from these rising
monuments to our great
misfortunes. Highways, street
corners, schoolyards, cafes,
churches, concert halls
packed with totems and tributes.

A lachrymatory
might rest on every
corner to capture our
tears backed by drumbeats from
funeral marches, prayers,
bagpipes, *Amazing Grace.*
Or will we finally
grow tired of our ceaseless

weeping, staring at
lists of our latest victims,
ringing our hands like
a chorus of bell-pealers.
Can we act to banish
memento moris,
to celebrate instead
those who are still with us?

Six minutes 20 seconds

*On March 24, 2018, Emma Gonzalez, a survivor of the Parkland, Florida school massacre, held crowds spellbound at the anti-gun March for Our Lives for six minutes, twenty seconds of silence – the time it took the shooter to kill 17 students and wound 15 others.

As Emma stands
resolute
before millions
crowds begin
to shift
uneasily
uncertainly
look around
feel how long it is
to wonder
as moments slip by
like lives lost
or altered
just how it would feel
under a desk
in a closet
covered in classmates' blood
surrounded by downed friends,
dead teachers
how it would be
to hear *crack crack crack*
from all directions
Emma does not move
she is still counting
each second
is a lifetime lost
she knows how
it will end

NEW MEXICO VISIONS: PRAYER FOR PULSE VICTIMS

On June 12, 2016, 49 people were murdered, and 53 others gravely
injured by a shooter at the Pulse nightclub in Orlando, Florida. Prior to
the shooting, the bar had been a safe place enjoyed by members of the
area's LGBTQ+ community.

Each orange rose copper mesa
surprises, as if radiance can be
whispered in code languages
known only to ancient spirits
who shape shift our route as we go.
Fragrant piñon and Russian sage
fill the air. Pale mauve, indigo,
sage mountains shadow us like
incandescent talismans who can
protect our day dreams or bring forth
memories soft as a wind song.
An afterglow follows us along
curvaceous high desert roads
like sparks of a new idea
or the sweetness of a first kiss.
As luminescence teases us along,
changing with each turn, we venerate
those cut down as they danced, kept faith
with youth and love. Perhaps they are
Raven now or Buffalo or Corn Maiden.
Or brazen cactus flowers, sprouting
out from thorns and scales to dazzle us
with illuminations of survival.

THIS IS WHAT MEMORY SOUNDS LIKE. PART I

the sounds of our madness (Las Vegas)

It sounded like firecrackers
said the witnesses and victims
as bullet-ridden bodies piled up,
followed later by medics, then candles,
flowers in white, yellow and red.

He was just a guy
said the shooter's brother
as he was hunted down at home by
news cameras and microphones
where he had hoped to hide instead.

Let's not talk gun policies today
said the president's press secretary
as she stared out from her lectern
and told us everyone was *sad*
and needed time to mourn the dead.

I really didn't want to die
said a concertgoer as he lay down
on the ground next to a lifeless man
whose days, like country music, had ended
in tales of heartbreak and bloodshed.

We saw nothing nefarious
said the hotel manager about the guest
whose suite held ten suitcases and twenty-three
weapons capable of dispensing death
from thirty-two stories overhead.

He passed all necessary background checks
said the gun store owner, opining
on the shooter's mental fitness
as he spoke to law enforcement,
assuring that he was not misled.

I can't get into the mind of a psychopath
said the sheriff as he tried to explain
how things could turn so swiftly,
as the lists of missing and injured
grew ever more widespread.

This is your life now
said the young neurosurgeon
to the newly quadriplegic
grandmother as she tried to imagine
the future as seen from her sickbed.

I cannot breathe anymore
said the new wife, whose medic husband
saved her life but died on the ground
before her, as she stared out at
the long arc of widowhood ahead.

TALLAHATCHIE HATE CRIMES

*Fourteen-year old Emmett Till's body was pulled from the waters of
the Tallahatchie River in 1955 after he was tortured and lynched. In
2008, the State of Mississippi finally installed signs chronicling his
kidnapping and murder. That sign was uprooted and thrown into the
river. A replacement was riddled with bullets. A third marker met the
same fate. In October 2019, a fourth memorial was dedicated. This
time, the sign was made out of bullet-proof materials.

Their mourning began
sixty-four years back, when Emmett's
brutalized body was first
dragged from bloodied, turgid waters.
His mother, defiant in her
fury of grief, made everyone stare.
She knew the power of outrage.
Look at my son, she demanded.
Dared them to look away.
See what your hatefulness has wrought.
Some were moved, some marched.
The young boy remained very dead,
his death spot unmarked apart from
memories of perpetrators and their progeny.

Anamneses is not enough.
Proof of life requires consecration.
One day memory turned to memorial
until it too was thrown into the Tallahatchie.
A second one was shot up like
its namesake. Then a third.
Vandalism is a hate crime,
says Emmett's cousin Ollie. She
recalls each scream that filled up her
childhood home like a freshly dug grave.
Still sees the body pulled from
roiling waters, frail against force of lead.
Memoir's weight still drags us downward.
Once again, his family gathers at the shoreline.

Grief has the worst manners

said my friend whose son jumped
from a building without
giving her warning
so she could have held him back
or laid herself down on that sidewalk
to cushion his descent.

Parkland is filled up with
churlish survivors.
They want to rewind
all the videotapes so
their rage turns poetic.
This is uncouth America.

All manner of tragedies
repeat, fold and unfold
like origami birds. Our heads
spin as we watch them take flight.
Wider wingspans sweep through air.

Scurrilous rhythms of newer sadnesses.
Murmurations of sorrow.
Failed medicines. Graceless faces.
Long guns. Short memories.
Grief has the worst manners.

IMAGINING A CONVERSATION ABOUT
THE UNFINISHED BUSINESS OF GENOCIDE

*During the 100-day period from April 7-July 4, 1994, over 800,000
Rwandans died as a result of ethnic-based violence by Hutus against
Tutsis. Over two million Rwandans became refugees and more than
400,000 were orphaned. Each year between April 4 and 11, Rwandans
observe a week of mourning, known as *Icyunamo*. Most genocide
victims were killed in their own homes and villages, often by their
neighbors. The remains of more than 250,000 victims are interred
at the Kigali Genocide Memorial Center.

Standing in Kigali now,
one might briefly forget
one hundred days of slaughter.
Memorial flames burn scarlet, gold, white.

We sip our proper cups of tea.
My daughters and yours
laugh as they play on the grass,
too young to remember.

Even now, all it takes
is a slight refraction of light
for blood and bones
to fill up our tidy yards.

You and I knew so many
of the hidden ones. My blinded cousin
walks on stumps.Your brother
dreams of his missing arm.

I watched my parents die in gunfire.
Perhaps your nephew pulled the trigger.
My uncle meant to save your sister.
Her fear crumpled him in the dirt.

The Genocide Fugitive Tracking Unit
still does its work. East Africa teems

with escapees and hunted people.
Forgiveness is a brazen conceit.

We examine its heft, fondle each fold
and strand, like a fashionable garment.
Each day we dare to don it, we close our eyes
for a moment before we walk into the light.

AN AGING IRA FIGHTER REFLECTS ON
BREXIT'S UNINTENDED MEMORY CONSEQUENCES

Borders are on everyone's mind these days.
Not just the ones where two-year olds
are stolen from their parents and sent
to courtrooms to plead their cases.

I'm thinking back to how the way one prays
could turn quite deadly if one strolled
down the wrong street, or someone's accent
might cause them to vanish without traces

of guilt spilt on men wearing soldier's berets.
I used to live in Derry's Bogside, patrolled
without end by those who aimed to prevent
our claims to history's rightful places.

More than most, I know there are multiple ways
for lines to be drawn. Then, as truth unfolds,
we seem surprised at first, before we lament
our decisions. Occasionally, we wonder if grace is

something solid to be retrieved. I am amazed
still at our will to oppose treaties to control
our destinies. At first, peace arguments
made us skeptics. We stared at those sad places

where rigid boundaries left us dismayed
and divided, household from household,
and our viewpoints stiffened in dissent.
We fervently believed that no place is

safe except the one that meets our gaze
with like-minded visions. As tales were told,
we often found it necessary to augment
details that would emphasize the basis

for the walls we built. Soon, malaise
transformed us. As barbed wire unrolled
to top our fences and gates, we vented
and raged while men with briefcases

drew up documents filled with clichés
that some judge would use to uphold
our divisions. Eventually, if we went
on this way, we would be locked in stasis,

staring out from colored passageways
of green or orange, martyrdom tales retold
until it was time for us to invent
new heroes to take up their places.

The Good Friday accord was praised
for pushing back against the grief we hold.
We hoped it would allow us to reinvent
ourselves after *the Troubles* had disgraced us.

I am not eager to return to those days.
I drive tourists around now. I've been long paroled.
Yet, my days on the blanket can still disorient.
Remembered tribal thoughts fill in bordered spaces.

THE WEIGHT OF SILENCE

*On Sunday, April 22, 2018, an ISIS-affiliated suicide bomber in Kabul, Afghanistan killed at least 57 and injured more than 120 people lining up to receive national identity cards that would allow them to vote in the country's parliamentary elections. Twenty-two women and eight children were among those killed. A neighborhood resident, Mohammad Kalgrim, told a reporter "I have carried so many bodies that I cannot even talk." Most survivors of the blast said they were no longer likely to cast votes. *New York Times,* April 23, 2018, A4.

Our dead lie entwined with ashes.
Like ribbons of faded hours, they
land in drainage moats where school
uniforms drift past like tiny boats
in muddy red waters. A small girl,
whose pink schoolbag becomes her pillow,
drifts next to her mother's body
hollowed out like a vessel.
A clerk, still holding forms, pencils,
lies bent at an odd angle, staring.

Once, the things we ferried
were cups of cinnamon tea,
books of ghazals, prayer carpets,
promises of prophets. We passed time
at windowsills or waiting in lines.
We pursued relief from lesser grief
like failures of imagination.
That Sunday, as firemen tried to wash
away the sins of our street corners,
we harvested slain neighbors like crops.

GOINGS AND COMINGS

I.

The ability to leave is tangled
into our genes. Did our ancestors
apprehend that there would never be time
to pack up anything of substance?

As the call snaked through village streets – *Cossacks
on the move* – who had chances to decide
about photographs or keys to locks? Jewels were already
sewn into hemlines, rubles pushed into boot soles.

Reach far enough back into any family's
story, there are always tales
of unwanted comings and goings.
A knock at the door. Everything changes.

II.

Sometimes, leavings can seem more innocent.
We imagine a sorting, a lifting, a closure.
We want to believe time always hovers toward return.
In such visions, we see ourselves standing

at familiar doorways. As we conjure *click*
of keys, hairs rise at the napes of our necks.
We step onto the threshold, throw open windows
to find our old lives dusty but otherwise intact.

But we know better. The truth is dark and spare.
There will be nothing left but memory.
There is no need to sort, sift, carry, no occasion
to cradle keys as if they were newborn babes.

MEMORY AGAINST FORGETTING

South Africa understood
our need for active memory.
At Lilesleaf, Mandela hid
until betrayal, trial, jail.
Now, liberation history
is spelled out along paths he walked
so people will always know how
to preserve their truest stories.

Here, in these un-United States,
the power of remembrance is in doubt.
Each day, falsehoods spill out like echoes.
Future chroniclers will no doubt be amazed
by the shadows cast by ghosted truths.
How we were asked to remember events
that did not take place. To unhear. To unsee.
Power's pronouncements shape-shifted daily.

We once believed in veracity, not false
versions of it. Our eyes were trusted guides.
Before too long, someone will design
a museum to enshrine not what was
but what was wished for. Authenticity
will be locked away, replaced by panoramic
pipe dreams, shiny trinkets that resemble
facts, alternatively remembered.

FOR WANT OF A TEST

what a beautiful memorial we shall build
  to all the kingdom's dead
    more than were lost   in Vietnam in Korea
    in Middle East misadventures
    in our formative war of revolution

more than   Galveston   Maria   Katrina
  Okeechobee Chenière Caminada
    bodies submerged   from wind and water
      then blooming like water lilies dug out from beneath
      tin timber bricks   as the land dried out

as death tolls climbed   governors pleaded for tests
  for knowledge   for supplies for accuracy for tracing
    charts revealed truths   our tests were faulty
      no one knew who was sick   until it was too late
      everyone was a carrier   or a victim   or lucky so far

one person's pneumonia   another's spring allergies
  false negatives   false positives   false promises
    some went about their lives   did not worry
      they believed in immunity   the optimism of youth
      the blood of Jesus   the luck of the Irish   wishful thinking

no country tested more
  crowed the general and his lackeys
    hospitals continued to fill   stretchers ferried new patients
      whose lung x-rays looked like milk glass
      whatever side they were on did not protect them

the nail   the shoe   the horse
  the rider   the message   the battle
    the kingdom
      maybe that will be the statue we erect
      near the emptied streets

Find someone like yourself. Find others. Agree you will
never desert each other. Understand that any rift among you
means power to those who want to do you in.

——from "Yom Kippur 1984" by Adrienne Rich

PANDEMIC YOM KIPPUR

More than two hundred thousand souls
will be missing from this year's Book of Life.
They will not hear the Shofar or rejoice
in the Days of Awe. Yet we must embrace
their memories as if we were bound by blood.
We must atone for their sins as if our own.
We will fast in their names and abandon
worldly concerns. Wear white. Give to the poor.
Pray that someone is paying attention
to our great need in these sorrowful days.
And when the fasting has ended, we will
honor their deaths with our solemn promise
that we will avenge these losses with
our poems, our voices, our marches, our votes.

IN PRAISE OF THE LACHRYMATORY

*A small vessel found in ancient Greek and Roman tombs,
believed to have been placed there to hold tears of mourners.

These days, every home
should have one.
Strategically placed by our
bedsides, in our kitchens.
There is no accounting for when
weeping might begin, unwelcome
as an uninvited guest, yet strangely
comforting once formalities
are dispensed with. It takes energy
to sob without stopping for breath.
This vessel will stave off need
to mop up regrets like oil spills.
Each dawn, we can water our lawns
with remnants of yesterday's anguish.

PART III:

THROUGH THE LOOKING GLASS

Remember your birth, how your mother struggled to give you form and breath. You are evidence of her life, and her mother's, and hers. Remember your father. He is your life also. Remember the earth, whose skin you are: red earth, black earth, yellow earth, white earth, brown earth, we are earth...Remember the wind. Remember her voice. She knows the origin of this universe.

— **Joy Harjo,** *Remember*

THROUGH THE LOOKING GLASS

Our angled bathroom mirror lets me
peek back into reflected DNA of lives
I barely know, doppelgängers whose
memories might emerge in my dreams.

Resemblance resides in ancient photographs.
My brother has gathered lists of family names:
Mulvennas, Mulvaneys and MacMaughs.
Masonheimers, Hopkins, Adams, Sweets.

And the ships that brought them over.
The ship Shannon sailing from Port of Larne,
shriveled potatoes littering the ground.
The famed Mayflower headed for Plymouth.

Farmers, Fishermen. Teachers, Judges.
Engineers, Artists, Writers, Surveyors.
Clerks, Secretaries, Soldiers, Lawyers.
Memories buried or star-scattered.

If we knew more, pride would not always
follow. Like our shaky-handed declarer
of independence who also owned slaves.
But what of lesser heralded lives?

Dusty census, tax records tend toward
the men. Peering into celluloid eyes,
it is hard to pinpoint much, but I believe
it was the women who kept it going.

Staring into silvered glass, I see
my mother. She looks a bit tired,
uncertain, restive even. As if she
finally intends to say what she thinks.

She never did speak up for herself.
Not like my Aunt Bess, determined

to address the world's ills in letters to
Congress. Speeches to strangers on

a trolley ride. She loved FDR and JFK.
Her language all wishful thinking,
certain of hope's triumph. Now, she
watches me closely for signs of rage.

My grandmothers stare back as well.
I never knew them and stories are slim.
Maude died young. One small child left crying.
Who knows what genetic stew she cooked up.

Grandmother Mary painted beautiful
canvasses. But not many and not for
long. Her husband shot dead in his office
for philandering, she put away her paints

and easels. Took in borders to feed five
children. Maybe she continued to color
masterpieces in her head while tending
to the needs of transients and émigrés.

In this recursive light, I faintly see
a shadowed image on the Antrim Coast.
It is circa 1793.
Widow of a fishing boat accident.

She sails westward with six children to
South Carolina – farther than imaginings
or prayers – a new life rises from the sea
even as fish call to her lost husband.

I study the surface of my hall of mirrors,
wondering at all the rest whose genes are
stirred and sifted. Are things as they should be?
Isn't there more to be seen?

RISE AND SHINE

It's time to Rise and Shine!
My mother's voice calls out.
I calculate minutes
left to me to wash up,

quickly dress, grab my books,
pens, papers and race toward
the aged yellow school bus
lumbering up our steep hill

like an unsteady drunk
on a rocky road home.
This is my strange new world.
From Seattle to small

Maryland farm. It might
as well be Saturn's rings.
Parents will make these calls
and never tell you why.

NOTHING is here! I cried.
Later, I understood
my mother thought the same
though she never said so.

She used to sit outside the
yard goods store bus stop.
She knew when it stopped
in town. Sometimes it makes

no difference where the bus is
headed as long as you're
on board. But she never did
get on. She came back home.

Made our daily meals.
Took in our tales of woe.

Got us up each morning,
her game greeting the same.

Later, I found a ticket
in her jacket pocket.
It was so frayed I could not
make out her destination.

HAPPY FATHER'S DAY

On Father's Day, I always remember
my mother. How she looked down rather than
speaking up. Her fear of failure not focused
on the man who undermined her
but on herself for failing to be worthy.
How she left home for him, her suitcase close,
as she stared out at farmlands, old churches,
barnyards from the train window.

As signs of her old life passed by her,
what promises kept her going? I've always
wondered about that man waiting for her
at a Texas depot. She told me he was
different than the one I knew later on.
Twice married and divorced, he must have known
how innocence can fade if not tended
like a newly seeded garden. Was he

kind first, gentling her fears? Did he laugh at
jokes in morning light, dance close at their
honky tonk bar named *Yellow Rose of Texas?*
How could she know when he left for war
that she had known the best he had to give?
And why did he return to sire kids
he did not want as he tired of demands set
by wishful thinking and civilian life.

I often thought of my parents as birds.
He, a hawk circling for some hapless
prey. She, cowering like a timid
chickadee afraid of her small shadow,
always fearing that she should have
done more, been more. Or, shrinking away
from limelight, bending toward safety
of corners like a nervous turtledove.

Their nest was always precarious.
It overflowed with psychic debris.
Once, she walked out our front door
wearing a dull brown hat with a small
side feather. She stared away when she
mumbled goodbye. I remember how my father
slammed the door behind her, then frightened us
by staying silent for the rest of the day.

RECALLING A FAMILY'S WINTER HIKE

Pain can make a person mean.
Maybe that explains my father.
No one ever knew what might set
off his fuselage of fury
on an otherwise humdrum day.
No one knew how to end his rage.

Now, I wonder if his spirit
was willing but his body not?
Or vice versa? Medications
never seemed to manage the carnage
or stifle the damage. We all
wanted to become pharmacists.

Once we went hiking. Mount Rainier,
amicable against morning light,
offered an omen of temperate
trails ahead. Hemlock tree lines
had been softened by light snowfall.
Velveted rocks parted as our

family wandered, listened for
blue grouse, jays, winter wrens, even
a woodpecker's *tap tap tap tap*.
Even now, I cannot recall
what set him off, howling wolf-like,
loud enough to shake powder from

white pine branches and shroud us all
in misery. Others passed us by,
eyes cast down as if they might
avoid our fate by pretending
we had vanished like red tailed hawks.
We stood very still. Misery's awkward

victims. I can see his plaid flannel
shirt, my mother's coat pulled tightly
to her, my sister's blue snowsuit,
inscrutable against the sky.
In a photograph, taken earlier,
we are all smiling in the sun.

REMEMBERING "TREES"

*Joyce Kilmer's poem "Trees" was first published in 1914. Kilmer died at the age of 32 in World War I. He wrote three books of poetry.

a poem as lovely as
a robin's nest as
a branch as snowy as
a mouth as
a limb as sturdy as
a breast as
a prayer as
a god as

joyce kilmer was
the first poet I ever
knew about
a rare bonding event
with my father
as we stood
in a pine forest
on a cold fall day

as I shivered
watched starlings soar
and colored leaves
roll around like fiesta marbles
my stern father began
to recite each word
soft sweet
like a flower seller

he had me repeat
each line until I knew
more than
I had ever known
about trees
or god
or the breathless magic
of poetry

ATTENDING A MOVIE OF OUR LIFE

We want our memories to be like movies.
Edges round and full, bathed in cinematic
sound. Dialogue filled with wit and warmth.
A John Williams score rising as suspense
builds, softening as angry words dissolve
to tender touch. Golden statues in reward.

One night in Ireland, my mother and I
were settled in before a stone fireplace.
Irish coffees steamed in tall glasses
on our well-used round wooden table.
The pub was darkened with history
yet somehow radiant, as if all the stories

shared there had cast their warmth
on the rough pine floorboards, layered
over the uneven horse plaster walls.
We were no exception. Warmed by
whiskey, freed from time, our
conversation stretched into the long night,

burnished by our recall of those
we had loved against others' odds.
We occupied the director's chairs.
Our scripts were epic. Perhaps we tinkered
a bit with casting, set design but we
were certain of the endings we desired.

BEQUEST

As the hospital aide wheeled her down
a darkened hallway for some midnight
scan, my mother handed me her

small blue topaz ring. *Here,* she snarled.
You'll get it anyway when I'm dead.
Before I could protest, they were gone,

the ring burning my palm, as if its
silver filigree setting had just
been removed from a soldering iron.

Later on, when she was back at home,
I offered it back, hoping she would not
remember the heat of the exchange.

She declined my gesture. Pretended
to be pleased that I would now enjoy it.
For all I know, she might have been

happy about its transfer. Maybe it
recalled the shine of times when we were
more like friends. When we exchanged books,

recipes, shopped for bargains, dined out,
laughed aloud at our own jokes. Before
she handed me her car keys or began

to wake in pre-dawn anxiety, learning
names of each EMT who transported
her to the hospital. Maybe I displayed

regret at our transition to far-flung
galaxies, our past alignments drifting
past us like so much space debris.

As I wear her ring each day, I see now
that it was a gravity-defying gift.
She is present. We are our best selves.

THIS IS WHAT MEMORY SOUNDS LIKE. PART II

It is so quiet, I could hear
a pileated woodpecker
miles away from my door.
I could float on stillness
as if I were a migratory bird
who has left earth's clamor
far beneath my wingspan.
I have disconnected all plugs.
Set aside newspapers. Nothing
reaches me now beside
sounds of my heartbeat
competing with din of memories.

1. the sounds of unmistakable laughter

I can hear my mother shrieking
with laughter across our tract house,
usually quiet unless my Dad
is home yelling. So I know this
is *Big*. No boundaries. It must
be hilarious. I run down the hallway
eager to be part of the fun.
I do not expect secrets
so her tightly closed bedroom door
surprises me. I have imagined

her face alight, waiting to share
the wonder of the joke, smiling at me
when I walk in, pulling me to her.
She will share this story that sucked
her up into its gay center, making ripples
in the air, each one a bit higher,
more breathless, overpowering our rooms.
I knock and knock, excitement
increasing with each rap
as I call out to her *Let me in. What is so funny?*

65

Eventually, her door slowly opens.
She stands, slightly bewildered,
her face colored pink
by shame and surprise.
She will not look at me.
At once, I see there is no joy here.
In the purity of her tears,
all witnesses were forgotten.
I am new to sounds of raw,
unmistakable sorrow.

2. *the sounds of limited options*

Sitting in a hallway phone booth,
stomach pitching with fear, I almost miss
my doctor on the other end of the line
saying *Congratulations!*
Unwanted tidings of joy –
though not unexpected after I had run
wild one night, breathing in
tangy scents of *Mexico's finest,* laughing
at inhibitions like they were little polite jokes
people stopped telling long ago.

I consider my limited options as I mumble
No, I don't need another appointment right now,
then hang up. Fellow students stride past me
toward class or lunch or study groups.
I feel the way one does when a loved one
dies – suddenly surprised when pieces
of the world remain firmly in place
no tear-streaked faces; no signs of fright
marked like a third eye on foreheads.
Though my *problem* will be solved, it will echo.

3. *the sounds that bruises make*

I cannot really recall blacks or blues.
It is more about the sound –

66

belt noises *swoosh swoosh swoosh*
through air as I ran or tried to run.
The clamor has been muffled
by time though my deep dreams
still sometimes fill with it –
Thwack! Thwack! Thwack!

Just the other day, that misery woke
from a busy city street as I waited for a bus.
My father is long dead. So too his raging anger.
Yet as I turned, I half expected to see him
standing nearby, arm raised in fury.
Instead, a man on a nearby sidewalk
clutching a white rope as it were a lifeline,
hurled it against his back. Its knotted ends
landed. Again. Again. Again.

This man's face is brown, bearded.
His black woolen cap almost covers
his ears and eyes, as if he cannot bear
to witness the damage. As if pain's
pandemonium carries no more weight
than a door loosed from rusted hinges.
Passersby and I look up at an anguished
hullabaloo mirrored in shop windows.

As he rages, I see leather whips, rods,
canes of birch filling spines of former
slaves with jagged scars that spread out like
sea urchin mantles or public squares
adorned by bloody backs of vagrants
as agony's din rises higher than prayers
to heavens. The rope still swings
as the bus pulls up and we board.
Thwack! Thwack! Thwack!
Perhaps he worships like the Flagellants,
seeking salvation by his own hand,
other avenues having failed him.

GRAVESTONES

We have walked with care
over bumpy sponges of earth.
Bright golden lichens sparkled
over headstones filigreed with moss.
In misty, salty afternoon fog, our trek
could be artistry as well as mystery.

We stroll by ancient abbeys,
silent sentries to casual visitors,
to centuries of forgotten souls.
Our search for buried history
is a mission, wildflowers
and soft rain notwithstanding.

We have been at this all day,
at towns' edges where faded
parish records hinted at names
near enough to make a churchyard
stop. As we stare at stone-filled grass,
Mickey, our guide, is first to find her.

She rests amidst a group of
crooked totems that lean without
order, crosses and angels crumbled.
She is "Mary Mulvenna,"
her faded name barely legible.
Newer graves are here as well,

bordered with flowers resting like
tiny birds. But it is Mary's stone
that I have come for. A history
visible to my naked eye
even if nothing more
can ever be known.

FLIGHT

How time does fly! everyone says.
Sitting down this morning with my
once upon a time stepdaughter,
I feel the flutter of those wings

as we navigate our past lives,
dissecting the journeys taken.
We steer clear of roads untraveled,
our own passages not so quick.

Peering backwards, our eyes shaded
from relentless memoir, we speak
of the mysterious ways love
can become a vanishing act.

We marvel at how migrations
always feel so uncharted, no
celestial messengers to set
a course for air-borne journeys.

Yet here we are. My hair turned silver.
She with two sons grown to men
the age I was when we said hello
for the first time. Now she's on her own.

Suddenly, I lose my taste for
talk of disappearances.
I take her hand, try to slow
down the velocities of time.

SALVATION AS SEEN BY THE BEHOLDER

My sister believes she can save everything.
One can barely navigate each room
for fear of tripping or dislodging piles:
books, stuffed animals, potted ferns,
art supplies, dog toys for her rescued cat
who weighs twenty-five pounds, his tail
twice the size of my foot. He towers
over us on a carpeted structure
meant to resemble a condominium
or perhaps an oak tree. *Look,* she calls out,
my strawberry plant is blooming. In her kitchen
hallway. On the last day of November.

Years back, she parted with all her
worldly goods. Joined a commune where she
shook away messy memories of family strife,
wishes for her future harbored by others.
We saw her rarely. Shrugged off tales
of her group leader's grand visions for
saving the world from us. One day she emerged
like a newborn. She began to curate
her new life with her neighbors' remainders.

She gathered refuse as if she were a
member of Howard Carter's team exhuming
shards of pottery from Tutankhamen's
tomb. Nothing was too worn to leave
behind. Each item cried for new life,
a chance to be restored. A broken branch
could house a painted icon, a fallen
owl feather from a felted hat could
rejuvenate a peeling red brick garden wall.
Old picture frames could hold new portraits.
No sin of misuse unforgivable.
Eternal life possible.

I'M DREAMING OF A WHITE CHRISTMAS

I heard the crash
all the way in our kitchen.
It was the snow globe,
you bought for us
to celebrate our first
Woodstock Christmas.
The black and white cat
wearing a Santa hat
still sat on her red armchair,
her once perfect glass orb
now shattered. Shards
lay scattered next to
tiny dots of fake snow.
Liquid oozed everywhere.
Who knows what it is
made of, what chemical
stew was soaking into
the bedroom's oak
floorboards. Our old cat
had looked a lot like
her tiny twin, though
she never expressed much
interest as the globe whirled
and the song jingled.

Yes – I yelled as the scope
of the mess expanded,
as you stood stranded,
shoes enveloped in
messy blobs of white,
holiday wrapping and
ribbons mixed up
with the debris.
I left to retrieve paper
towels, a broom,
a plastic refuse bag.

When I returned,
you were still staring
at the jumbled sight. Fuming.
Outside, real snow glazed
over everything. Even
broken branches looked
magical in a wintry
slant of light. Not so
indoors where sparkles
were in shambles.

What a holiday metaphor –
how many broken
pieces have we swept up
in our thirty years? How many
vials of glue or rolls of tape
have we employed in hopes
of salvation? As we stood
mid-wreckage, unsure
how rescue might emerge,
a familiar song suddenly
slipped out from the trash –
the music box's tiny roller
and pins jarred back to life.
Suddenly there was
a promise of some hope
that a glistening day
might still lie ahead – *just like
the ones we used to know.*

TICKER TAPE

I hope I remember
everything I need to
return to when it
is too late to venture
outside   when it is too
dark   or too risky or
too uncomfortable
maybe just too tiresome
to call it all back up
like so many Dewey
decimal system cards
turning pale yellow in
the back alley tossed there
once the library went online

I know I don't want
the sordid stuff of
bankers boxes that rested
like aging warriors
in our basement
calendars tax returns
drafts of articles notes
of meetings memos to files
leaflets calendars flyers
shrinking down turning brown
a shredder truck shuddered
one afternoon in our alley
as we watched it all
morph into party confetti

What I want to recall
is how you loved me
how we drove to Cooper Lake
as trees turned to copper
and russet   how we

stared into the water's
mirror as if we might
watch our story play out
before we had to live it
on dry land   how I took
your hand and decided
to alter the parade of my life
how lucky we are to be able
to celebrate each other

DACTYLOGRAPHY

*Dactylography is the scientific study of fingerprints.

DaVinci's inky brown
thumbprint was recently
found at Windsor Castle.

A parchment sketch, a woman's
body, near her left arm.

Imagine the moment –
cadaver splayed beneath
him. As he shifts paper,
grasps it with his thumb,

perhaps he peers closer,
to see if her face might
warrant a sketch as well.

Last night I placed my
thumb against my wife's arm.

No remnant of that moment
remained. Yet I want to
think she would remember
that stroke as if inked there.

When we are gone, no one
will know or care about
this act. Mona Lisas

we are not. Or Minoan
potters. We are just us.
One random touch
brushing against decline.

SNOW DANCING AT MIDNIGHT

backlit snow flirts
against dark skies
circles flutters   swirls
like meteor showers
or surprised sparrows
miracles are expected
of us when angels
pirouette laughing
in frosted midnights
they dance
against darkness
mingle like fireflies
as light and movement
interweave
among deep thoughts
sometimes sparks
explode
against blackness
so deep
we cannot fathom
our decline
cannot focus
our sights
on true north

in this immaculate
auditorium
where our hushed
audience drifts past us
we can re-evaluate
everything
which dream
gave us pause
which sharp regret
sped us toward
ancient galaxies
which memory

76

should vanish forever
press your finger
against my lips
so I do not spoil
this night of
frozen carousels
it is so quiet
I believe we could
hide in our meadow
as drifts pile high
and re-tell our story
as if it was new

DEBATING THE MERITS OF CONFESSIONAL POETRY

No one has any use these days
for confessional poetry
says the poetry professor
who is guiding us through epochs
towering with symbols, laden
with mythological meanings.

Though he did not mean anything
personal, I can feel the heat
as it rises up from my neck
to my cheeks. As if he knew each
word I had written down just before
we gathered for our weekly session.

Sylvia Plath, Sharon Olds, Anne
Sexton. Your blood-smeared pages make
everyone nervous. We take our
glasses of Scotch or Chardonnay
and stare out over a garden
fence. Suddenly, we know ourselves.

Maybe nobody cares what we write
back in our rooms papered in yellow,
set apart from the routine and rote,
but you granted us permission
to strip away all artifice,
to shout *Fire* in crowded theatres.

It is not all Bedlam. Surely,
another's anguish can be quite
instructional. Medicinal.
Let's take that trip down memory
lane and see who survives unscathed.
Aren't we each reflected in our flames?

PART IV:

WHO WILL BEAR THE WEIGHT
OF WHAT WE HAVE KNOWN?

It's a hard time to be human. We know too much and too little.

— Ellen Bass, *Like a Beggar*

MEMORY GAMES

remember bumblebees, butterflies and bald eagles
remember snail darters
remember wolves who roamed through snow
  before Yellowstone's boundary lines
  became a death sentence
remember elk and moose
remember buntings, blue jays, a blue footed booby,
  condors and crows, sparrows, scarlet tanagers
remember pilot whales, manatees, dolphins, orcas
remember silvered seals
  their babes floating on icebergs
  when icebergs were large enough
  to be seen in the distance
remember when the color red reminded you
  of cardinals, not fire engines
remember gorillas in mist, how we knew
  their names and names of those who loved them
remember koalas, wombats and kangaroos,
   dunnarts, potoroos, green carpenter bees
  and black cockatoos

remember the first swig of water you took
  from a plastic bottle
remember the first time you drove
  your car to a gas station to fill the tank
remember when your dad sprayed *Roundup*
  on the grass so it would look like velvet
remember when hair spray was amazing
remember when Paris was not blazing
remember when Kansas was not drowning
remember when Paradise was not a
  burned down town in California
remember when the Amazon was a forest
  filled with rainbows called orchids
remember when a moon landing
  caught everyone's attention

even though we hardly went back again
remember when the world
  could be navigated in 80 days
  and Jules Verne sank us   breathless
  20,000 leagues beneath the sea

remember when we thought the future
  was always going to lie ahead of us
  or at least some of us
remember when optimism was a luxury
  and memory was not a losing game

you might think this contest
  has gone on too long
even if you're tired of playing
remember how much more is lost

ON MEMORY'S LAST DAY

> *...a day is coming one will not recall, the last day of everyone's life, and on that day one will oneself become as irrecoverable as all the days that have passed ...One will no longer be present at the universal morning roll call.*
>
> ——**James Baldwin**

Each day now, this is what we fear
most: the plague reaches us as we
sleep like innocents. No escape.
No time to offer apologies
to all those who might wish to hear
us feeling sorry for ourselves.

We have never had much control
over finality. Usually,
our story ends outside our will,
despite our best intentions.
Choice is that rarest of finales.
Timing almost never perfect.

Obituaries no longer
read like mystery stories. We
know both cause of death and killer.
Some unlikely microscopic
parasite, so small a grain of
salt could be Everest by its side.

Television screens are filled with
pictures of grey balls afloat, pierced
with cinnamon hued crown-like spikes.
To keep them away, we wash our
hands like obsessive compulsives,
spray our surfaces with alcohol.

We take our temperatures daily,
maybe more. Venture out as if
we were cloistered nuns or lived

where burqas were required attire.
Yet no one knows how this disease
will strike. Or who. Or when. Or where.

And so we huddle behind walls
and doorways. Clap our hands to cheer
on those whose luck required them to
be out in the hurricane's eye.
We try to marshal memories
to save us if we reach morning.

RINGS OF FIRE

*The Laboratory of Tree Ring Research at the University of Arizona,
Tucson, founded by astronomer A.E. Douglass in the 1930's, studies
connections between sunspots and climate reflected in tree rings and
cores. Half a million samples fill the lab. As trees age, the rings
circling the trunks expand each year. Each stores data about a year's
temperatures, precipitation, jet stream behavior, fire activity and other
extreme climate events. Tree rings contain elements of carbon which
reflects the interaction of cosmic rays and nitrogen at various points
during the tree's history.

Tree rings turn out to be nature's
Dear Diary. They can tell us when rain
refused to end and when it stopped its fall.
Like Johnny Cash, forests know how
fast a heart can break, how heat
of fire can *burn, burn, burn.*

A Bosnian pine tree named Adonis
has stood in Greece for a millennium.
It speaks to jet streams, hears star secrets.
In Colorado, a twenty-year drought sets
records as river waters evaporate.
Blue spruce chronicle their migration.

When volcanoes blew their tops or desert
climates pushed north like arid armadas,
bristlecone pines recorded each maneuver.
As nomads scattered like their failed crops
of corn, beans and squash, their exodus
story was written in concentric coils.

A chiaroscuro of cosmic rays
and solar flares dance across Japanese
cedar tree circles. They carry messages
as prescient as ancient Anglo-Saxon
Chronicles or Dead Sea Scrolls. Collapsed
empires etched, like poetry, in grains of wood.

We tumble into burning rings of fire while
our ancient chroniclers turn pale as shadows.
As they watch everything go *down,*
down, down, narrative no longer captures
our descent. Flames rise higher. Metaphor
vanishes. Next, meter, rhyme. Then memoir.

SANCTUARY

*On January 29, 2020, the body of Homero Gómez González was
found floating in a well near the El Rosario Monarch Sanctuary in the
Mexican village of El Soldado. González had spent decades working to
preserve the Monarchs and protect the environment in the Michoacán
State.

I was not always a lover of butterflies.
Once I was a logger, clear cutting these pine
forests like those who later turned against me.

One autumn morning I saw conifers tremble
like young brides, heard sounds that pierced my innocence.
I understood then that my job was to save them.

How can such tiny creatures travel three thousand miles?
I queried them as they shivered, shimmied there,
circled around each limb like jeweled bracelets.

For two months, sunshine is their compass as they fly.
They come to rest here in our pines. Skies thicken with orange,
yellow, white laced with black. My silhouettes of autumn.

No one prayed as hard as me for their safe arrival.
They write their memoirs in these deep woods.
It is their great-grandchildren who will return next year.

Sometimes I stood at the edge of the tree line to listen
to their angel sounds. Each synchronized wing beat calmed me.
It was like heaven, if one believes in such magical thinking.

I felt such sorrow when their arrival began to thin down,
turn translucent, like a memory that fades when we most need
it to be sharp. I craved vivid images of sunlight at rest.

When the end was near, I pleaded for mercy. Not for me.
My expendability was always understood. For my floating
charges whose safety is all we have left as refuge from ourselves.

REQUIEM

Pollinators have lost their taste for life.
No longer piping like Pan, our humble
honeybees have grown quiet, tired perhaps
of warning us about our survival odds.
Their soft *buzz* drifted away into light.
Dancing bees left their audience in silence.

At first, we did not worry much. Lilacs,
yarrow, goldenrod continued to bloom, cone
flowers bent over in breezes like lines
of chorus girls. *It's just a cycle*, we
said, giving due credit to Mother
Nature's knack for the mysterious.

Bees cannot detect danger's color red.
It is ultraviolet light that draws them
toward the rose, a light we cannot see.
As our collective memories shrank like
late August gardens, hives emptied like echoes.
Now we begin our chant for the repose of lost souls.

THE FIRE THIS TIME

Desert boundaries shape shift like werewolves.
Sometimes, they move slow as a seed unfolding
to blossom. Other days, it happens quick
as a knife slash or a Bedouin tent
folding at dawn. Even in rain, oases
shrivel up like belated apologies.

Saharan sands will surely land in Kansas.
As they expand to every crevice,
sift through kaftans across continents,
settle in hair and eyes, will we all sink,
parched, blinded, survival skills swept away?
Before too long, we could become Mars.

As fables are told, retold, voices slip slide
across barren ground, nestle in cracks
grown wide as riverbeds. *We never saw it
coming*, someone claims as dust drifts down
from ancient stars to lands where villages
once glistened under rays from a red sun.

The lightning has shown me the scars of the future.

—W.S. Merwin, from *The Nails*

My broken magnolia tree

has already begun to shrivel.
Two buds, still impossibly pink, remain
half-opened on its downed branches
as if startled from deep dreams.

At its roots, lime green suckers
gather like a curious crowd
at an accident scene, relieved
to have escaped calamity.

The trunk's break is ragged. No hope
of new growth, no chance at repair
or rebirth. The suckers linger on
like hopeless causes often do.

My friend tells me he can dig out
the remains next time he comes by
to mow our lawn. My optimist's memoir
had craved a different denouement.

Years back, this same magnolia suffered
a lightning strike. Halved, hunched over,
it nonetheless kept growing. Its garish
gash grew gnarled and thickened to bark.

Each summer it reached a bit higher, stood
a bit straighter. Juncos and chickadees launched
their arias astride its glossy green leaves.
Some years, it was twice ringed with magenta flowers.

Such perseverance pleased me, proved
invincibility was still possible against grim odds.
Magnolia blossoms were among earth's first petals.
Imagine the secrets they might hold.

Who can ever know the full weight
of grief? When it can no longer
be borne, does it shape shift to new
dimensions or simply tumble to ground?

*The human immune system contains T and B cells, known as lymphocytes, that can make antibodies to fight invading pathogens like viruses. Working in conjunction with NK ('natural killer") cells, they form memory cells that remember the same pathogen. Once detected, they determine the most rapid and effective response to fight future infections.

If I Can't Remember Everything

then please let's focus on
memory cells so my
immune system can get
busy, arm itself for
warfare, don night vision
goggles, start to track down
viral threats hidden in
secret pathways, trying
to avoid capture.
Repatriation is
on the agenda once
we locate the leaders.

Wanted: emigrés gone rogue,
transplants with survival
skills, activists railing at
barricades. One hopes for
victory as searchers
head out. Faded maps lie
crumpled in their pockets,
edges torn. They are looking,
magnifying glasses fixed,
for bent twigs, tattered scraps,
muddy footprints, coded
words in unknown languages.

Or what about muscle
memory? What would we
pick if choices were ours –
an errant word, a lost
name, a misplaced number

or the bicycle ride,
as our hair sailed behind
us like Isadora Duncan's
silken scarves? My mother
remembered how to do
the Fox Trot long after she
forgot who taught her to dance.

ADRENALINE RUSH

Before our fears hovered on every face
(when we were brave enough to step outside),
I am trying to remember what it was like
to hug someone, to reach out for a hand.

When we were brave enough to step outside,
strangers stepped away. Even if they wanted
to hug someone, to reach out for a hand,
we all knew that distance was required.

Strangers stepped away even if they wanted
to save our souls or talk about blessed days.
We all knew that distance was required.
Our desire for so much more was ravenous.

To save our souls or talk about blessed days,
how we ached for contact, revered its rush.
Our desire for so much more was ravenous –
how our cortex lit up like a candelabra!

How we ached for contact, revered its rush!
Someone needs to look back at what we craved –
how our cortex lit up like a candelabra –
at the memory of touching each other.

Someone needs to look back at what we craved:
the tantalizing thrill of adrenaline
at the memory of touching each other
before our fears hovered on every face.

LAMENTATIONS

The thieves are crying in the wild asparagus.

—Robert Bly, "POEM"

If we are lucky, someone is crying
outside the boundaries of poetry.
Perhaps they've stopped to stare
at brazen lapis butterflies who hover
above a bush exploding with flamingo
pink flowers while their wings
turn late afternoon's fevered air into
echo chambers. Our eyes moisten as trees
pale, pare down to naked branches.
As wingbeats still, some tears begin to fall
for memories of frivolous summers
when we believed in invincibility.
Today, grief spills out for childhood thefts,
lost caresses. We weep for colossal mistakes
constructed on sands of good intentions.
Is it too late to confess our sins, to seek
forgiveness in the names of others?
It is too late to wrap ourselves in the comfort
of magical thinking once sorrow has risen
on the plains of stolen memories?

AMNESIA FOR A DAY

A friend recommended this remedy
for grief. Better than sleep, she said.
All thought, memories wiped away
like blood from a crime scene. Forget
every being you have ever known.
Then you cannot lose them or be
lost in mourning's hollow heartbeat.
No more Madonna halos aglow
with survivor's guilt. Once removed
from any life one has lived, names
devolve to statistics, become
random obituaries gone to
coffin, urn, hallowed ground, dust.
We have no need of tears. We remain
whole, unscarred. Strangers on foreign
shores. Freed of need to recognize
faces or follow familiar tales,
we drift like space debris, stare
at each passing constellation
as if its stories might soothe us.

AN ORDINARY DAY

*New York City's Hart Island has been the site of burials for the poor, the unknown, prisoners and stillborn babies since 1868. It is believed that more than one million bodies are buried there. Since the COVID-19 pandemic, gravediggers have been at work seven days a week burying victims whose families have not claimed their bodies. *The Washington Post,* "New York City's Family Tomb," April 27, 2020.

About suffering they were never wrong…

—W.H. Auden, "Musee de Beaux Arts"

The Governor has reported on today's
statistics. Hospital entry lines flat.
Deaths remained below four hundred two days
running. Grieving loved ones no longer
wait for news, watch their screens for hopeful signs.
Someone has gathered up the last effects.
A mortuary has been contacted.
Family members notified. No one knows how
to plan virtual farewells. How to pick out
coffins on zoom. Cherry, oak or pine?

It seems like just yesterday when mourners
gathered amidst wreaths of white carnations
and red chrysanthemums. When casserole
dishes of meat and cheese were delivered
at sunset. When reminiscences were
drafted, sympathy notes written, poems
about grief pulled from dusty volumes,
rehearsed in front of bathroom mirrors.
When the power of a group hug could light
up a metropolis. When shoveled dirt

could fill more than a gravesite. No one wants
to mourn alone. It may be harder than
a solitary death. As morticians try to create
virtual farewell artistry for luckier survivors,
others grieve without video comfort.

Grave-diggers dressed for space travel
place the unclaimed dead in trenches
on Hart Island to join legions of lost souls.
Each day, a saltmarsh sparrow leaves
Long Island Sound to pay last respects.

ON FINDING A BIRD'S BROKEN EGG BY THE
SIDE OF THE DRIVEWAY ON A MORNING WALK

A flash of color that
could easily be the
blue of Bahamian
seas lies beached at a
corner, beneath tall pines.
Only half of the split
open shell remains,
as if it had surfaced
like a shipwreck's flotsam.

My story — a baby
thrush, eager for a first
taste of air, has kicked out
of its shell, burnt orange
belly pulsing — vital,
noisy, feather fluffed.
Not the other story
where hunter met prey,
fate littering the ground.

In my tale, red hawks recede.
Optimism is the wingbeat. New beaks
open wide, feathers form.
Chicks fledge, launch. One fine fall
day, they embark on their
Mexico journey where
some small respite is savored
before they sail back home,
safe in pre-dawn memories.

SAY THEIR NAMES: AN ERASURE POEM

black and brown women go missing too
but not everyone counts them   or says their names
red lights flash at them as much
they get stopped as much   profiled as much
they get followed as much   forgotten as much
dissed as much   harassed as much

they die too

  for their bad luck   for their bad timing
  for walking   driving   shopping   answering the doorbell
  for crying   running   partying   hiding
  for their boyfriends   for their girlfriends
  for their asthma claustrophobia   PTSD
  for their depression   dementia   diabetes
  for being a victim   for calling 911
  for being angry   for being hungry
  for being afraid   for being fearless
  for refusing to put out a cigarette
  for not having a lawyer   for not getting a phone call
  for being a working girl   for not having a job
  for not conforming   for not complying
  for speaking up   for speaking out

just for the hell of it
just for the ease of it
just for the history of it
just because no one sees them
just because amnesia is everywhere
just because no one says their names

LaShanda Anderson   Tamisha Anderson   Sandra Bland
Rekia Boyd   Ma'Khia Bryant   Eleanor Bumpurs   Miriam
Carey   Alexia Christian   Michelle Cusseaux   Deborah Danner
Shantel Davis   Sherida Davis   Latandra Ellington   Janisha
Fonville   Shereese Frances   Jessica Gonzalez   Mya Hall
Meagan Hockaday   Kendra James   Atatiana Jefferson

Charleena Lyles   Kathryn Johnson   Aiyana Jones   Patricia
Kruger   Iretha Lilly   Stephanie Lopez   Natasha McKenna
Kayla Moore   Rosann Miller   Tyisha Miller   Frankie Ann
Perkins   Sheneque Proctor   Tiffany Rent   Jeanietta Marie
Riley   Alberta Spruill   Denise Stewart   Angelique Styles
Breonna Taylor   Loreal Tsingine   Jessica Uribe   Sonji Taylor
Anjuli Verma   Tarika Wilson   Jessica Williams   Melissa
Williams   Alteria Woods   Maria Rita Zarate

THIS IS WHAT MEMORY SOUNDS LIKE. PART III

the sounds of music when birds have left us

> *Between 1970 and 2019, more than one in four birds in the United
> States and Canada have disappeared. Research published by the
> journal *Science* examined population losses due to human-altered
> landscapes. Among the vanished birds were millions of blackbirds,
> finches, larks, blue jays, warblers, sparrows, orioles, bobolinks,
> grosbeaks and juncos.

Three billion birds have disappeared
like proteins gone missing
in a brain. Cross every fourth
species off the list.

The Cetti's Warbler
whose trill inspired first notes
of Beethoven's Second, its last
movement filled with dainty chirping.

Or Mozart's starling, said to have
inspired his Seventh Piano
Concerto. And ascending larks,
as inscribed by Ralph Vaughn Williams.

In Respighi's *Pines of Rome,* a
nightingale dazzles. Now there are fewer
song sparrows, blackbirds, doves,
whooping swans and finches

to echo wind serenades.
Where will music go
when we stand beneath empty skies?
When memory no longer holds birdsong?

SEARCHING FOR SOLACE
AT THE COUNTY FAIR

Does anyone remember when a trip
to the county fair allowed a view into
lives we might want to try on? They were
plain as leather boots, solid as a Holstein,

robust as a lime green cantaloupe striped
gourd sitting like a Buddha astride
a wooden table, blue ribbons leaning in
like prayerful monks. Once we could swirl

upside down strapped into a rusted
can that only pure faith could elevate,
laughing alongside strangers whose stories
of longing resounded much like our own.

This year it feels like everyone's hair is
laced with lightning bolts and we all have lit
matches in our hands. Kind of like Medusa
except that all of us have turned to stone.

LIFTING COSMIC VEILS

*At the end of January 2020, NASA ended the work of its Spitzer
Space Telescope after sixteen years of receiving images of stars,
planets, galaxies and other celestial wonders from its telescope. Using
infrared instruments, the telescope operated like night vision goggles,
sensing heat radiating from celestial objects. Among its discoveries was
that of nebulae IC417, known as "The Spider and the Fly," several
earth-like planets in the Trappist-1 planetary system and the Pinwheel
galaxy. *The Washington Post*, February 4, 2020, E2:"NASA Shuts
Down Spitzer Telescope."

I've got my eyes on you.
I peered in where no one
has traveled. I stared through
yesterday's combustions too.

The cosmos teases us.
So much history there.
Some of it displeases us—
its violent atmosphere—

but most vistas amaze.
We were watching our past
twist, tease, flicker and blaze.
An artist's canvas so vast

generations will not
comprehend its visions
until they're an afterthought.
I've sent you collisions

no one remembered,
seen inside dust storms,
tracked stars that resembled
spiders and their prey, forms

of fury and feral
interplay that could stop
armies, turn atoms sterile,
cause volcanos to pop

and oceans to appear
where only sand had thrived.
Now no one wants to hear
these tales, see what survived.

My infrared travels
charted new asteroids,
saw planets unraveled,
found pinwheels inside voids.

Maybe you knew my worth,
truths I could tell
as I drifted past earth,
knew it does not end well.

SEARCHING PAST SINGULARITY

*Black holes usually form when stars collapse and die. Gravitational singularity exists at the center of most black holes – a one-dimensional point which contains a huge mass in an infinitely small space where density and gravity become infinite and space-time curves infinitely. Scientists can only see black holes by noticing light and objects pulled towards a single point. In a sense, they only can see the black hole's gravity when they notice the black hole.

Some days it seems as if
our missing memories
must have fallen into
celestial black holes.
(The ones astronomers
report on from fancy
telescopes in desert
bunkers and mountaintops.)
Imagine them sucked in
like a giant breathing
exercise, then swallowed
whole instead of exhaled.
We gasp for air, as they flail,
fall, burn. Collapse is total.
Once vibrant, awash in
prisms of light, deep with
meaning, we can sometimes
track their decline, watch as
they spin like dancers toward
center stage before they leap
out of sight. One instant
is all that is required
before we are stranded
near their vanished flame.

The greater mystery is
how not every memory
falls away. We wish we
could control their journey.
Some we would happily

dispatch into the abyss:
each careless word that stung
like a face slap, every
failure to act as we knew
was demanded, times we
turned away from needs we
might have met, withheld a
gentle touch or spoke too softly
when rage was required.
If prayers to Mnemosyne
mattered now, we would seek
the muses' help with thoughts
that curved inward and were
lost to gravity. But time
erases without regard
for cravings or regrets.
Hollowed at the edges,
warped by wishful thinking,
our astral search continues.

WHAT IS HERE

Perseverance
has landed today
on Mars.
Curiosity will have company.
Everyone is eager for news:
Red cinnamon rocks.
Long dead grey lakes.
Dust filled grooves.
Caves chiseled into canyons
like a Henry Moore garden.
Layers of mystery
embedded in swirls of rock
marbled as a fine steak.
We are always looking
for something
to make sense of.
Something that explains
our odd and quirky selves,
the reasons we love and lose,
fight over nothing sensible,
torture and torment.
We are always looking
for history,
for memory,
for stories,
for permanence,
for renewal.
The deeper we dig,
the less happy we are.
So we fly off
to other realms
hoping to learn more
from long dead planets.
Hoping there is something
new under the sun.

WHO WILL BEAR THE WEIGHT
OF WHAT WE HAVE KNOWN?

I. Memory is not the same as memoir.

If we could stand every disappeared
memory in a line-up, how would that
transform our future selves? Or does our brain
do us great favors by sorting, sifting,

revising, deleting like Maxwell Perkins
working late into a night? Perhaps
the red-penned version prepares us for
surprises, keeps our secrets ready for battle.

A South African museum promotes
"the memory against forgetting" as it
showcases Mandela's revolutionary
life. So we all know what may be required.

II. Heat is not the same as light.

I remember watching television
as Thích Quang Duc turned to fire. Flames soared
like prayers, obscured the figure folded
like a lotus blossom. He told no one

of his plans before driving into Saigon,
gasoline can jostling in the back seat.
Afterward, only his heart remained.
The light he sparked spooked everyone

as if we had all lit the match.
Today, truth's incandescence will escape
unless we pay close attention to smoke
clouding the mirrors to our burning world.

III. Statistics are not the same as truth.

Keeping tabs on the dead has always been
a disorderly business. Body counts often
depend on who is doing the counting.
And why. Take Hurricane Maria, where

sixty-four bodies have now been joined by
three thousand more. Or, COVID-19
where cases triple only when someone tests
for illness. The volume overwhelms us.

I remember searching for my father's
gravestone at Arlington amidst marbled rows.
I wondered how many names were not listed,
survivors left to weep in anonymity.

IV. Escape is not the same as departure.

Some days you can almost hear the keys
click in the door no matter how far
from home you are. Other times *home* is nothing

more than wishful thinking. A muddy floor,
a few blue tarps or scraps of plastic cloth.
There are tented refugee camps in which
generations have come of age as they

waited for documents, counted cash.
I remember my mother, dressed in a
suit and hat. I was ten. She stared down when
she said goodbye. Her return surprised me.

V. Recovery is not the same as healing.

Hospital hallways fill with those for whom
faith is redefined by clock ticks and surgeon's
turn of phrases. Tubes and monitors provide
an alternate memoir. Nurses morph to Greek

choruses near bedside stages where waiting
becomes its own epic tale. For many,
pain's dull roar dims down as drugs dance
through eager veins like garage band groupies.

But fear always hovers: an errant cell,
a backfiring car, a rogue virus strain.
A Parkland survivor takes her own life.
A Sandy Hook father does the same.

VI. Velocity is not the same as power.

Sometimes one can feel the wind of forward
motion. Rush of speed, thrill of vanished
gravity. No need for Elon Musk to send us
spiraling toward distant planets.

We want to control our destinies.
Fists airborne. Knees on ground. Attention paid.
Selma's Pettus bridge. Stonewall. Standing Rock.
Harriet Tubman covered miles of darkness,

reading signs as if they were braille-pierced sonnets.
Her wary passengers inhaled for hours,
clung together. Frederick Douglass told us:
march, shout, fight, vote, write. Demands must be met.

VII. Touching is not the same as feeling.

Perhaps there are no random acts of violence
or kindness. Perhaps we are all guilty
for failures of nerve, memory lapses
and leaps of faith. Maybe we just need to

grasp the hand of the aging woman, her
worldly goods on grocery carts, as plastic
bags anchor the sides like buoys. You can
see she once was beautiful. Some days,

her hair woven into a careful braid,
she rests near a trash bin to read a book
of poems or stories by Henry James.
Other days, she is shrieking into wind.

VIII. Reasoning is not the same as understanding.

Most people agree that the longer one
lives, things that remain unknown expand
each cloudless night like mathematical
equations or long dead stars.

Scientists keep tabs on far afield black holes
and explosive events. They stare through giant
lenses, lean in to sounds from past lives we
will never know, send robots to scoop up

rocks from arid plains in hopes of learning
what we might have been or might have saved.
I still believe someone will one day detect those
routes, dig up the scrolls, decipher their codes.

ACKNOWLEDGMENTS

**Thanks to the editors and readers of the publications
where the works below previously saw the light of day:**

Twisted Vine Literary Magazine (December 2015): DIAGNOSIS;

MERGING STAR HYPOTHESES (*Finishing Line Press* 2020): RINGS OF FIRE, DACTYLOGRAPHY, REMEMBERING TREES;

Slippery Elm Literary Magazine (June 2019): TRAVELS TO THE VALLEY OF LOST THINGS (First Place 2019 *Slippery Elm Literary Magazine Poetry Competition*);

An Apple In Her Hand (*Codhill Press* 2019): SIX MINUTES, 20 SECONDS;

The New Verse News (2018): THINKING ABOT YOU; AN AGING IRA FIGHTER REFLECTS ON BREXIT'S UNINTENDED CONSEQUENCES; THE WEIGHT OF SILENCE;

The New Verse News (2019): WHEN BLACK HOLES COLLIDE;

Red Planet Magazine (Fall 2019): THE FIRE THIS TIME;

The Write Place at the Write Time (February 2016): GRAVESTONES;

The Voices Project (June 2017): FLIGHT;

Junto Magazine (Vol. 3,Issue 4 December 2018): Portions of the poems THIS IS WHAT MEMORY SOUNDS LIKE, PARTS I-III first appeared under the title REVERBERATIONS;

The Write Place at the Write Time (Fall-Winter 2017): NEW MEXICO VISIONS: PRAYER FOR PULSE VICTIMS;

The New Verse News(2020): SANCTUARY;

Writing in a Woman's Voice: HAPPY FATHER'S DAY (June 22, 2020); UNSUBSCRIBE (September 27, 2020);

Albany Poets (2020) My broken magnolia tree (Honorable Mention, 2020 Steven A DiBiase Poetry Contest);

Poetry Leaves Anthology (Volume 5, Waterford Township Public Library 2020) *Poetry Leaves* Exhibition): WHAT IF EVERY FALLING LEAF WAS SOMETHING WE WANTED TO REMEMBER?

Hamilton Stone Review (Spring 2020): LIFTING COSMIC VEILS;

Songs of Eretz (Spring 2020): TICKER TAPE;

Platform Review (Arts by the People) (Spring 2021): IN THE END, WHAT DO WE WANT TO KNOW; THE FIFTH DIMENSION

The Poet's Billow (2019 Atlantis Award): MACULAR DEGENERATION (previously titled RANDOM ACTS OF BLINDNESS)(Semi-Finalist);

Willowdown Books (2020): *Poems for the Lockdown: An Anthology:* ADRENALIN RUSH;

City Limits Publishing (2020): *Poems of Political Protest: An Anthology:* SAY THEIR NAMES: AN ERASURE POEM; First Place Winner, 2020 Poems of Political Protest Poetry Contest;

New York Society Library (April 1, 2021): WHAT IS HERE (National Poetry Month
2021 Video Reading);'

Aji Magazine (May 2021): DISPATCHES FROM THE MEMORY CARE MUSEUM.

The Poet's Billow (WHO WILL BEAR THE WEIGHT OF WHAT WE HAVE KNOWN? (July 2021); Finalist, 2020 Pangaea Prize.

Thanks to the following friends and fellow creative spirits:

I am grateful to the gifted poet Charlotte Pence, whose editorial insights and support made this a stronger collection. I also appreciate the members of my wonderful circle of women writers – doing creative business as The Hudson Valley Women's Writing Group: Colleen Geraghty, Kit Goldpaugh, Eileen Howard, Tana Miller, Jan Zlotnik Schmidt and Kappa Waugh. In particular, thanks to trusted reader Jan Zlotnik Schmidt for her valuable commentary on these pieces and to my sister Elizabeth (Anastasia) O'Melveny for her technological savvy and creative ways with computer layout, book cover concepts and web sites. Last but not least, a special shout out to my dear friend Mary Gawronski, who has encouraged my post-retirement poetic adventures and served as trusted reader, informal editor and stalwart supporter over a lifetime.

ABOUT THE AUTHOR

Mary K O'Melveny lives with her wife, Susan Waysdorf, in Woodstock New York and Washington DC. After retiring from a distinguished career as a labor rights lawyer in New York City and Washington DC, where she represented workers, labor unions and political prisoners, Mary returned to writing poetry – an interest she had not pursued since college. Mary's poetry has been published in both print and on-line journals and anthologies, including *Aji Magazine, Allegro Poetry Magazine, Auroras and Blossoms, Coastal Shelf, FLARE: The Flagler Review, In Layman's Terms, Into The Void, Light Journal, Split Rock Review, Slippery Elm Literary Journal, Songs of Eretz, The New Reader, The Offbeat, The Voices Project, The Write Place At The Write Time, Twisted Vine Literary Journal, Voice of Eve* and *West Texas Review.* Mary's poetry has also been featured on national blog sites such as *The New Verse News* and *Writing in a Woman's Voice.*

Mary is a member of several writing organizations, including *The Hudson Valley Women's Writing Group* whose recently published anthology, *An Apple In Her Hand,* is available from Codhill Press.Mary is a Pushcart Prize nominee. Her poetry has received award recognition in national contests and competitions, including First Place in the 2017 Raynes Poetry Competition, First Place, 2019 Slippery Elm Poetry Prize, First Place, 2020 Poems of Political Protest Contest sponsored by City Limits Publishing, Finalist 2020 Anthology Magazine Poetry Prize ("Highly Commended"), Finalist 2020, 2017 Pangaea Prize sponsored by The Poet's Billow, Finalist 2018 Tom Howard/Margaret Reid Poetry Competition sponsored by Winning Writers, Honorable Mention, 2017 Tom Howard/Margaret Reid Poetry Competition, Semi-Finalist, 2019 Atlantis Award sponsored by The Poet's Billow. Mary was short-listed for the 2018 Fish Publishing Prize. She is the author of the poetry chapbook, "A Woman of a Certain Age" and a poetry collection "MERGING STAR HYPOTHESES" (Finishing Line Press 2018, 2020). That book was a semi-finalist for the 2019 Washington Prize sponsored by The Word Works.

Mary's web site is: www.marykomelvenypoet.com.

Made in the USA
Middletown, DE
18 August 2021